Other books by George Grotz

*Instant Furniture Refinishing and
Other Crafty Practices*

Antiques You Can Decorate With

*The New Antiques: Knowing and
Buying Victorian Furniture*

The Furniture Doctor

From Gunk to Glow

*Staining and Finishing
Unfinished Furniture
and Other Naked Woods*

Staining and Finishing Unfinished Furniture and Other Naked Woods

Being another manual of Deceit and Trickery designed to make you Master of the Colors in your own home . . . along with Expert Directions for Applying Finishes over Stain . . . Bleaching out your Mistakes . . . some Unvarnished Truths about the Wax and Polish Racket . . . and Scurrilous Directions for making Instant Antiques . . . all submitted with the usual False Humility . . .

George Grotz
"The Furniture Doctor"

Dolphin Books
Doubleday & Company, Inc.
Garden City, New York

Dolphin Edition: 1973
Originally published by Doubleday & Company, Inc.
in 1968

"Oh, what a tangled web we weave,
When first we practice to deceive!"

FOR MY WIFE

Sometimes I love her more than money itself.

Preface: The Inside Dope, or How to Think About Staining

Gangway, all you obfuscators of truth and reason, the Furniture Doctor rides again! Now I'm even going to tell you how to *think!*

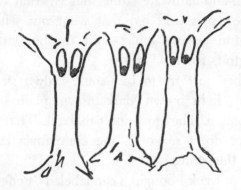

These are naked woods, of course.

But no fooling! If you want to learn how to stain and finish furniture, you've got to have the right attitude toward the job. You can't expect magic to pop out of those cans they sell you these days. Oh, the stuff in them is all right. In fact it's great. It's the directions that kid you along. They make it sound like child's play, and suddenly there you are, treading where angels fear to wade.

What I mean is that knowing the principles is what counts. And if you know them, you don't need step-by-step directions; you can think for yourself and do things differently, according to what you want out of life. After all, each manufacturer has his own can to sell, and he isn't going to be bothered telling you about what the other guy has in his can that will do things better.

As a matter of fact, most labeling is so bad that you *have* to think for yourself. For instance, I have yet to buy a can of stain labeled "Mahogany" (in an ordinary paint-and-hardware store, that is) that didn't turn out to be some wild red that went out with Martha Washington sewing tables—and maybe with Martha Washington, for all I know.

And then just try to buy some brown stain—brown mahogany, light brown, dark brown, plain brown, any kind of brown. They just don't make it. That is, the big companies don't make it, the companies that supply most of the stores.

Only last week I bought a can labeled "Penetrating Oil Stain—Non-bleeding." Well, it didn't bleed, all right—because somebody had poured about a cup of varnish into it, which made it colored varnish, as I understand the English language.

And there is a lot more, as you well know if you have been messing around with this home-craftsman business for long. But now you are saved. Reading this book will make you an instant expert. Well, at least you will know what you are doing for a change.

There's another thing.

If you thought your Christmas was a mess, you should have been at our house.

Because of the wide variation in materials—and how they are labeled—you can't take every word I say as gospel truth. You've got to learn to try things out on little scraps of wood. Or, even better, on the backs of drawer fronts and the bottoms of tables; this way, you will have exactly the same conditions you will have when you start working on the fronts of drawers and the tops of tables.

Now for the most important part of all.

Let's not be wild-eyed dreamers. Let's stick to thinking in terms of the possible. You can do an awful lot with stains, but there are exact limitations. So let's get it straight right now what can be done and what can't.

Pine is the best wood for staining. It takes the stain

evenly, and you can get a light tone or a dark tone of any
color you want. You can make pine look like almost
anything: fruitwood, cherry, maple, mahogany, walnut—
even pine. But you can't make it look like oak or hickory,
because these two woods are distinguished by their large,
open pores. Of course, you can stain a pine piece to
match the *color* of some oak piece so that the two will
look alike from across the room in a dim light. But that's
about it.

Of course, this isn't much of a limitation, because
most of us can live without oak or hickory. And we can
all be very happy that practically all unfinished furniture
is made out of pine. And there it is, sitting in all those
stores waiting for us to make it into whatever our hearts
desire. Also the same kind of pine can be obtained in any
lumberyard. Just ask for ⚹1 shelving pine. The ⚹1
means that it has very few knots. The ⚹2 grade will
have a knot about every eighteen inches, which is fine if
you like knotty pine. This is what I use when I'm making
a fake cobbler's bench or other rustic piece. For a cup-
board or even for built-in shelving, you might want to
pay the extra money for ⚹1 grade.

So pine is fine. Where we begin to run into a little
trouble is with the colored woods, such as cherry (reddish) and walnut (slate brown). With these, your stain
must add to the present color, making it redder or
browner, as I explain in chapter 9, "Staining Dark
Woods." It is also possible to bleach the natural color
out of these woods, so that they are almost as light as
pine when you have some special need for making them

so. This is discussed at the end of chapter 6, "Bleaching Stains Out."

Now for the real limitations on staining. Some woods are so hard and dense that they will absorb only a small amount of any stain. These are maple, oak, hickory, chestnut; almost as bad are the pale fruitwoods, such as apple and pear, though you don't run into these very often. To make these woods dark in any color, about the only thing you can do is to cover them with a film of lacquer or varnish that contains a lot of stain. We have a chapter on how to do that, too (chapter 8, "Staining the Hardwoods").

So that's how you have to think about staining. Like a reasoning person—that's all. That's not too much to ask, is it? Try, anyway. It may be the turning point in your life, and it might improve all your interpersonal relations.

As always, good luck in your life!

George Grotz

Contents

PREFACE: THE INSIDE DOPE, OR HOW
TO THINK ABOUT STAINING   11

1. PREPARATION OF THE SURFACE   23

   Depending on whether the piece is store-bought, stripped, dipped, sanded, or scraped.

2. MIXING STAINS   29

   To get sophisticated colors or exact matches to pieces you already have.

3. KINDS OF STAINS   35

   . . . and how to apply them. Besides the usual oil stains, you may someday want to try the sealer stains, the alcohol stains, spirit stains, and good old Minwax.

4. THE END-GRAIN PROBLEM   43

   How to get an even tone on porous surfaces such as the ends of boards.

5. SEALING STAINS IN   45

*In case you are an old-fashioned craftsman
who doesn't believe in sprayed-on finishes.*

6. BLEACHING STAINS OUT   47

*In case you change your mind or slop it on too
strong on your first try. (Also bleaching naturally dark woods.)*

7. STAINING PLYWOOD   53

So it doesn't come out looking like a flat zebra.

8. STAINING THE HARDWOODS   57

*Such as maple and oak, which are so dense it's
hard to get much stain into them. (But where
there's a will, there's a way.)*

9. STAINING DARK WOODS   61

*Such as walnut, mahogany, and cherry. Any-
body for teak, ebony, or rosewood?*

10. APPLYING A SHELLAC FINISH   65

*The virtues and shortcomings of "old reliable"
and the varnish makers' lie that you can't varnish over it.*

11. APPLYING A VARNISH FINISH 69

Five easy steps to a perfect varnish finish—which means alcoholproof—if you'll promise not to read the directions on the can.

12. APPLYING THE SPRAY-CAN FINISH 77

As in Instant Furniture Refinishing, *which is another book entirely.*

13. LINSEED OIL AND ALL THAT
and JUST PLAIN WAX 81

(Two chapters in one—a Grotz Double!)

14. THE GREAT WAX AND POLISH
RACKET 85

Concerning all that baloney you see on television about "lemon oil" like Grandma used to use and "feeding the wood"—for which you'd need to have holes in your finish. Or your head.

15. INSTANT ANTIQUES 89

Where the worm holes come from, and other aging techniques that fool 'em every time.

*Staining and Finishing
Unfinished Furniture
and Other Naked Woods*

1. Preparation of the Surface

Depending on whether the piece is store-bought, stripped, dipped, sanded, or scraped.

AS the old song went, it ain't whatcha do, it's the way thatcha do it. And when it comes to staining, the way that we do it is with a little thoughtful care in the beginning—which will make all the difference in the end.

This applies even to an unfinished piece of furniture that you have bought in a store and that would seem to be quite ready to start on. The main thing to consider is that the edges of these pieces are usually pretty sharp, and pine is such a soft wood that the edges will get little dents in them through common use after the piece is stained and finished. Obviously, this will happen to a much lesser degree, and will be less noticeable when it does, if the edges are rounded a little. It is called taking the curse off the edges, and you do it with fine sandpaper, rubbing slightly across the grain at first, and then with it.

On squared-up modern pieces you will want to take off only a sixteenth of an inch. With pieces in the Early American style you can go as far as you want, if the rounding hasn't already been done or if you are working with new wood from the lumberyard.

Another point to consider is that lower-priced unfinished furniture usually has a surface that is fresh
from the planer, and it may still show the marks of the
revolving planer blade. In this case the whole surface
should be sanded evenly, so that the stain will go on
evenly. If you don't sand it, the stain will make the marks
of the planer blade more noticeable.

Now let us look at pieces from which an old finish has
been removed. If it has been sanded, well and good. It is,
in effect, brand-new wood, and all you have to do is
check it over carefully to see that all the sanding was
done with the grain, so that across-grain scratches
won't show up when your stain goes on. If you find
any, just sand them out.

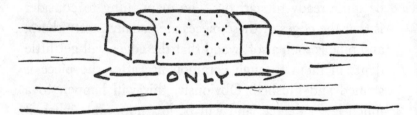

*I never will understand why they go on making sandpaper
when it is so bad. Production paper lasts ten times longer,
which makes it cheaper in the long run, too.*

If the finish has been removed with a scraper—which is
the case sometimes with antiques from the backwoods,
where some old duffer thinks he can't afford sandpaper
—you might want to sand the surface smooth, so that
the marks of the scraper don't show. If you do, the work

will go a lot faster if you buy "production paper," which lasts a lot longer than sandpaper, and wrap it around a block of wood. This stuff is available now in all hardware stores both in sheet form and in little rolls fitting into plastic holders that are really handy and work well. "Production paper" lasts longer because the grit used is glued to the paper better than the sand is glued to the paper in sandpaper.

If a piece has been dipped in some caustic solution to remove the previous finish (and fourteen coats of paint), the surface will be soft and hairy, and in this case I think the best thing to do is to scuff it smooth with a medium-grade steel wool and stain it. I suggest this because the dips not only make the surface hairy but also tint the surface of the wood under the hairs, and if you break this surface anywhere you are going to have to sand off the whole piece if you want the surface to color evenly.

If you have removed an old finish with paint remover and rough rags or coarse steel wool, you want to be sure you have gotten all the remover out of the cracks and crevices. The removers that you wash off with water are the best, in my opinion, because water is cheap. The cheaper benzine-type paint removers (cheaper than water-wash removers, that is) have to be carefully scrubbed off with mineral spirits or lacquer thinner, or both.

The only other thing I can think of to worry about is the dust from the sanding. If there is a vacuum cleaner around, I like to use it going forward to suck the dust in, then going backward to blow the dust off the piece. But for a really great job of dust control try making an old-fashioned tack rag.

Fifteen years in a mayonnaise jar is tacky indeed.

Take an old handkerchief or small piece of towel and wet it with varnish. Squeeze it out as hard as you can. Then wash your hands and squeeze it again inside another piece of dry towel. This will give you the stickiest, tackiest rag you ever saw, and when you wipe a sanded piece off with it, it gets *all* the dust. I knew an old woodchuck who saved one of these rags for ten or fifteen years, keeping it in an old mayonnaise jar with the lid screwed on tight. Just thought you might like to know.

COMPATIBILITY CHART
(Just to avoid any confusion from the beginning)

THINGS THAT THIN WITH ALCOHOL	THINGS THAT THIN WITH MINERAL SPIRITS (or turpentine)	THINGS THAT THIN WITH LACQUER THINNER
SHELLAC — a finish that will also re-dissolve in alcohol at any time	OIL PAINT ENAMEL COLOR GROUND IN OIL LINSEED OIL VARNISH VARNISH STAIN (colored varnish)	BRUSHING LACQUER SPRAY-CAN LACQUER easily wipes off with lacquer thinner
POWDERED STAINS These are aniline dyes for wood	OIL STAIN	POWDERED STAINS often started with alcohol
LIQUID SPIRIT STAINS (from Behlen & Bro. or Constantine *)	SEALER — penetrating wood sealer, that is, clear or colored	SHELLAC—just as good as alcohol
*See chapter 3		LIQUID SPIRIT STAINS just as good as al-cohol *

2. Mixing Stains

To get sophisticated colors or exact matches to pieces you already have.

WHAT I'm going to tell you now is how to mix stain in any color you want, using only three basic colors of stain and a couple of drops of black or white oil color once in a while. Ridiculous? Not at all. Just think of all the colors you can mix with red, yellow, and blue! The only difference is that we are going to use three colors of stain that roughly correspond to red, yellow, and blue. They are red mahogany stain, maple (which corresponds to the yellow), and walnut for the blue. If walnut doesn't look blue to you, you are just going to have to believe that there is plenty of blue in it. Don't worry. Have no doubts. Follow me.

Now, since I know what a bother it is to try to read directions with your hands full of sticky brushes and cans, I have drawn up a table (pages 30–31) for easy reference. It will also keep you from getting my book all stained up from leafing through pages to find the paragraph you want.

But first a little advice about procedure. Naturally you are going to need a lot of newspapers for the floor and your mixing table; also rags for wiping the stain on

HOW TO MIX
SOPHISTICATED COLORS TO STAIN
PINE OR OTHER PALE WOODS

(See chapter 9, "Staining Dark Woods.")

USING EASILY AVAILABLE OIL STAINS

Thin with mineral spirits only!

OAK	MAPLE	MAHOGANY	WALNUT	BLACK	WHITE
YELLOWISH TAN	ORANGE	RED	BLUISH BROWN	COLORS GROUND IN OIL	

BROWN MAHOGANY

Start with a cup of walnut, add a teaspoonful of maple and two drops of red mahogany. Adjust to taste.

FRUITWOODS

To a cup of oak add a teaspoonful of walnut and a few drops of maple.

ANTIQUE BROWN

Two parts of walnut, one part of maple; add oak by the teaspoonful for lighter shades.

HONEY MAPLE

To a cup of oak add two teaspoonfuls of maple and half a teaspoonful of walnut. You may want a little more maple.

MODERN WALNUT

To a cup of walnut add a teaspoonful of oak, a teaspoonful of maple, and a quarter teaspoonful of black. For some shades add more black.

CHESTNUT

To a cup of oak add a teaspoonful of walnut.

BLOND

Start with half a cup of oak thinned with half a cup of mineral spirits. Add a few drops of maple and half a teaspoonful of white.

EBONY

Squeeze half a tube of black into half a cup of mineral spirits and add half a cup of walnut. For harder woods, leave out the mineral spirits.

TEAK

First stain the wood with a base mixed of equal parts of walnut, maple, and red mahogany. Maybe go a little easy on the red mahogany. Then streak with half a tube of black mixed in half a cup of mineral spirits.

DRIFT WOOD

To half a cup of mineral spirits add a tube of white, a teaspoonful of black, and a teaspoonful of walnut. Add more white if this looks too dark for your taste.

BROWN CHERRY

To two thirds of a cup of walnut, add one third of a cup of red mahogany and two teaspoonfuls of oak.

RED CHERRY

To two thirds of a cup of red mahogany add one third of a cup of walnut.

DARK OAK

To a cup of walnut add oak by the teaspoonful until desired shade is reached.

CEDAR

Two parts of red mahogany to one part of maple — thinned a lot with mineral spirits.

OLIVE

Mix the shade desired with color ground in oil, thin with mineral spirits, rub into wood, wipe off hard.

OLD RED MAHOGANY

The real Honduras mahogany is what the red mahogany stain was originally made for. Use it straight.

ROSE WOOD

Stain wood with straight red mahogany, then streak with black as in teak above.

PECAN

Two parts of oak to one part of walnut is the shade I like. Some use more oak.

SPIRIT, POWDER & SEALER STAINS

The proportions given above are for oil stains only. They only may work with other kinds of stain, because the different colors are often stronger or weaker than oil stains are. So start with very small quantities and adjust as needed.

and sometimes wiping off the excess after you have brushed it on. You will need some small mixing bowls or cans for your test runs and some regular cans for your final mixture.

The small cans for test mixtures are about the most important items in the world. They are for making teaspoonful-type test mixtures to try out on the backs of drawers and bottoms of tables and chairs. The test mixtures will enable you to make sure your mixtures aren't a little too dark or too light for your taste or for the match you are trying to make. Perhaps the chestnut you are trying to match will lean a little more toward the basic maple color than the usual shade that my proportions will give.

Be sure of your proportions before you mix your final batch of stain. And throw away mixtures you don't like. If you start adding first this color to correct that one, and then that color to correct the other, you have a ticket to disaster and will end up with a gallon of Early Nothing.

The table, "How to Mix Sophisticated Colors to Stain Pine or Other Pale Woods," was worked out for "penetrating oil stains," with mineral spirits as the thinner, because these are the stains most readily available at hardware stores, paint stores, and lumberyards. The black and the white are little tubes of "color mixed in oil," available at the same places. Actually, any flat black or flat white paint will do, in little eight-ounce cans.

The proportions apply to any kind of stain, and in the next chapter I'll discuss the other harder-to-find kinds and where to find them, if you want to get into this business all the way.

3. Kinds of Stains

. . . and how to apply them. Besides the usual oil stains, you may someday want to try the sealer stains, the alcohol stains, the spirit stains, and good old Minwax.

AS should be obvious to the meanest intelligence—as an old math professor of mine used to say—the way to apply stain is to brush it on and wipe off the excess with a soft rag. But there is a little bit more to it than that, so let's discuss each of the stains separately—since they all work a little differently and have different advantages.

PENETRATING OIL STAINS

The main advantage of the penetrating oil stains is that they are the most commonly available. They are dyes dissolved in mineral spirits or turpentine, which for our purposes are interchangeable. (Mineral spirits are cheaper.) This means that if your stain is too strong, you can thin it with mineral spirits or turpentine. It also means that if, after wiping the surplus stain off your wood, you would like the tone still lighter, you can slosh either of the thinners on and then wipe a good deal more of the stain out of the surface of the wood.

Another important advantage of penetrating oil stains is that they are very easily bleached out with

Clorox or any other liquid laundry bleach. But wait until the stain has dried out, which takes about fifteen minutes. Anyway, see chapter 6, "Bleaching Stains Out."

Most penetrating oil stains are clear, but some have an opaque pigment, which settles to the bottom of the can. Generally speaking, you'll want to leave the opaque pigment right there on the bottom, because it tends to obscure the figure of the wood. On the other hand, obscuring the figure of the wood may be just what you want to do. In that case, of course, mix the sediment in with the clear liquid.

The disadvantage of the oil stains is that they tend to "bleed": when you brush varnish on them, the varnish picks up the stain, and as you brush it around it gets blotchy. The cure for this is to seal the stain into the wood with a thin coat of shellac—three parts of denatured alcohol to one part of shellac. After the shellac is dry, proceed with whatever finish you had planned (see later chapters).

ALCOHOL STAINS

The alcohol stains are harder to find but well worth the effort. For one thing, they usually are found in very good colors. They come in small envelopes and are aniline dye powders of incredible strength that you mix in denatured alcohol to make your stain. There is no definite proportion, and you'll just have to experiment. But just to give you an idea, one envelope may make as much as a gallon of medium-strength stain, depending on the color. Some colors are much stronger than others.

The great advantage of the alcohol stains is that they dry almost instantly—as fast as the alcohol evaporates. Besides not having to wait for them to dry before you apply your finish, you can apply additional coats for darker shades very easily.

The alcohol stains will bleed into shellac or varnish if these are brushed on, and so they must be sealed into the wood by a sprayed-on coat of lacquer from a clear-spray can. Any clear, quick-drying spray will be lacquer, regardless of what the can calls it. The Krylon sprays are old standbys, and the line can be had in any art-supply store if you are in doubt about what your paint store carries.

Incidentally, you can, alternatively, dissolve some of these stains in water; don't, because water raises the grain of the wood. Also, after you have initially dissolved them in alcohol, you can thin them with lacquer thinner.

Finally, the alcohol stains in good colors can be obtained already dissolved in alcohol from good dealers. One good dealer is Albert Constantine & Son, Inc., 2050 Eastchester Road, New York, N.Y. 10461. That's in the Bronx, baby.

SEALER STAINS

The sealer stains are finishes in themselves. They have the consistency of varnish but sink into the wood —after which you wipe off the excess. When they have dried, you can simply apply wax or varnish over them. They are really good, strong finishes. They come in colors, which can be mixed in the same way that penetrating oil stains are.

From the point of view of staining, the problem is that you can't bleach out a sealer stain if you change your mind. You'll have to sand an eighth of an inch off the surface of the wood. So, really, the stains are a combination stain-finish. Good, but not really just a stain.

VARNISH STAINS

The varnish stains are colored varnishes—varnishes with stain in them. Unlike the sealer stains, they tend to sit on top of the wood; you don't wipe the excess off after application, but let it dry to a tough protective film—as with clear varnish.

Like any varnish, the varnish stains thin with mineral spirits or turpentine. They can be applied to give a darker tone to wood that has already been stained and sealed—or given any final finish.

On naked wood they act like a sealer stain—except that you don't have to wipe off the excess. And you can apply additional coats on a clear finish over wood so stained.

Their disadvantage is the same as that of the sealer stains—you can't bleach them out of raw wood, and you have to resort to machine sanding.

LIQUID SPIRIT STAINS

The liquid spirit stains are the equivalent of the powdered aniline dyes already mixed in alcohol. But they are superior in that they have been strained, have a reasonable and uniform intensity, and come in intelligent col-

ors of brown that are equivalent to modern tones
such as brown mahogany, Swedish walnut, honey maple,
brown cherry.

You apply them as you would an oil stain, except that
you thin them with either denatured alcohol or lacquer
thinner. They bleach out with liquid laundry bleach as
easily as an oil stain does. You can get them by mail
from Albert Constantine & Son (the address is on page
38).

They are available also, over the counter, at H. Behlen & Bro., Inc., 10 Christopher Street, New York, N.Y.
(near the crossing of Eighth Street and Sixth Avenue.
They call Sixth Avenue "Avenue of the Americas" in
New York, but any avenue that is between Fifth Avenue
and Seventh Avenue is still Sixth Avenue to me!).

MINWAX

This product, Minwax, gets a free commercial. The
formula is secret and all that, but the way I see it,
Minwax is a thin-bodied sealer stain—or a penetrating oil
stain with a little bit of some kind of sealer in it to
keep it from bleeding when you brush a finish over it.

Of course, the Minwax people don't want you to put
a finish over it: they say, Just wax it. This works out fine,
because the Minwax keeps the wax from sinking into
the wood and leaves a lovely dull-glow kind of look,
especially on paneling.

But when you use Minwax as a stain on furniture,

you will probably want a finish over it, especially a varnish coating on the tops of tables and bureaus.

Minwax gets a high rating from me for three reasons:

1. It can be bleached out without heavy sanding. (See chapter 6, "Bleaching Stains Out.")

2. It comes in some very nice colors.

3. While you can't get it everywhere, it is very widely distributed.

I've observed that the varnish- and stain-manufacturing businesses are localized ones. Many companies distribute their products over very small areas. Some of these companies have managers who aren't color blind, and so they produce very good colors—a really brown mahogany, for example, instead of the usual stupid mulberry red. It will be well worth your while to stop by all the paint and hardware stores in your area to check out their stain cards. You might save yourself a lot of messy mixing.

4. The End-grain Problem

How to get an even tone on porous surfaces such as the ends of boards.

SOME people couldn't care less about the end-grain problem, but some people eat with their fingers, too. And to both of yez, good luck. For us refined folks who do care, I am pointing out that the board ends of any wood—especially pine—will suck in stain like a sponge and therefore get much darker than the sides or running edges of the boards.

The way to stop this from happening is to soak the ends of the boards with a mixture of equal parts of clear ("white" as opposed to orange) shellac and denatured alcohol (usually sold as "shellac solvent" under some trade name). The job has to be done carefully, with a small water-color brush. Any shellac that gets onto the sides of the boards must be sanded off with fine sandpaper.

Now, when you have applied the stain and wiped it off, the end grain will be *too light*, because the shellac has kept the stain out. With a piece of fine sandpaper, simply sand the end grain lightly and wipe some more stain over it. A little of the stain will be able to get through the shellac, and the tone will be a little darker.

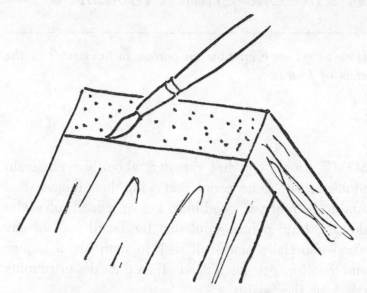

When you care enough to do your best.

Just repeat the sanding and staining until the end grain matches the sides.

Use production paper if you can get it, rather than ordinary sandpaper, because it will last so much longer.

5. Sealing Stains In

In case you are an old-fashioned craftsman who doesn't believe in sprayed-on finishes.

THE problem is this. When the oil or alcohol stains are applied to wood, the wood often won't absorb as much stain as you would like, and you won't get the degree of darkness you want—if you wipe off the surplus. Whereas, if you could leave that surplus on the surface, the color would be just what you want.

The answer, of course, is to seal in the excess by spraying it with a clear-spray can. Then you can build up the finish with additional coats of clear spray. Or, after the first coat of clear spray, you can brush on a coat of varnish—thinned with a littler mineral spirits or turpentine for easy, smooth brushing. But do not even *try* to brush shellac over the clear-spray coating, because the alcohol in the shellac will dissolve the spray coating and you'll have a real botched-up mess.

That is the situation with regard to sealing in the oil or alcohol stains. However, all oil-stained wood should receive a coat of brushed-on shellac before you apply a varnish. This is true even if the excess oil stain has been wiped off with a soft rag, which is the usual procedure. The reason for brushing on shellac is that varnish will actually pull the stain out of wood, but shellac won't pull it out, or allow varnish to do so, if you just brush it

FINISHES
Lie on top of the wood.
These are:
  SHELLAC
  VARNISH
  VARNISH STAIN
    (colored varnish)
  LACQUER
    (out of spray cans)

OIL STAINS
ALCOHOL STAINS
SPIRIT STAINS

Sink into surface of
the wood, coloring it.
(Can be bleached out
If no finish is over them.)

SEALER STAINS

Sink into and
HARDEN surface of
the wood besides
coloring it. (Can't
be bleached out
Surface must be
machine-sanded off.)

on and don't scrub it around. The shellac should be thinned with an equal amount of alcohol, maybe a little more, but not excessively as is so often indicated on the cans.

Naturally, this sealing in of the stain applies only to the oil stains (usually labeled "Penetrating Oil Stain") and the alcohol-solvent stains. One of the advantages of using a sealer stain or varnish stain, or Minwax, is that, once dried in the wood, they are stable. (See chapter 3, "Kinds of Stains.")

6. Bleaching Stains Out

In case you change your mind or slop it on too strong on your first try. (Also bleaching naturally dark woods.)

I had an Irish grandmother once who, after a long day at the hot stove, would say, "God bless the man who invented beds!" Personally, I prefer a hot bath—or a winter in Mexico. But among life's little delights, I think bleaching out a stain is right up there with the best of them.

There you are with this terrible mistake in front of you. You thought your wife said cherry, when she really said walnut. Or she said cherry, and you were supposed to know that she meant walnut. After all, after twenty years you're supposed to know she can't tell the difference between red and brown. Like how many times have you had to tell her—oh, forget it. There you are with your (?) great big solid mistake. And all you have to do is dip an old brush in a bowl of Clorox (or any other liquid laundry bleach) and with a few bold strokes return the wood to its original color. I mean, how many times in this life do we get a second chance like that?

All right. Enough of this highfalutin philosophy; let's get down to cases.

One of life's little delights. But you'll have to read the text to find out what it is.

To begin with, all stains are made of aniline dyes, which somehow or other people get out of coal. And all aniline dyes disappear when you hit them with sodium hypochlorite crystals dissolved in water. And, happily, sodium hypochlorite dissolved in water just happens to be all that most liquid laundry bleaches are. Nothing else—just that. And these are available under many different names all over the country. The most widely advertised and distributed is good old Clorox. But anything else that looks and smells and bleaches like Clorox is really the same thing, as you will see if you read the teeny-weeny print on the labels that you aren't supposed to notice.

For two bucks you can start your own "Clorox" factory.

(The reason for the print being teeny-weeny is to stop you from going to a chemical-supply house and for two bucks buying enough sodium hypochlorite to bleach California.)

Of course, after you have used the Clorox, you have to wash it off the wood and let the piece dry thoroughly. To be safe, it is best to rinse once with plain water, and then with about a quart of water into which you have poured two cups of vinegar. This will neutralize all traces of the bleach left in crevices. After the piece has dried, you are ready to stain again.

Sometimes the water will raise the grain of the wood, and you will have to scuff or lightly sand down the surface with fine production paper.

Incidentally, this process will also work on a factory-made piece of furniture that you have stripped down and on most antiques. I say "most," because some old furniture is stained with substances like berry juice that nobody has yet found a way to eliminate once it has soaked into the wood. Also the black streaks on some false-grained pieces won't come out either.

NATURALLY COLORED WOODS

If you are a fiend for very light colors or 1930 Blond (you poor thing!), you are going to be troubled with the natural color in woods such as walnut, cherry, and mahogany. These natural tones can also be removed, but the process is harder and more expensive. Bleaches are made for the purpose, but you won't find them everywhere, and the best places to look for them are good lumberyards where they do millwork as well as selling paints, varnishes, and so on. If they don't have them in stock, these places can order them for you.

The bleaches come under many brand names, but the man will know what you are talking about if you want the "one and two" or "A and B" kind of bleach. They come in quarts and gallons, and in glass bottles because one of them is an acid that would eat through tin. And, obviously, you are also going to be stuck for a pair of rubber gloves.

I've used these bleaches only a couple of times, but they really work well for people whose taste is all in their mouth.

This is either an electric Chevrolet or a belt sander.

In the interest of completeness I should mention here that no bleaches will work on sealer stains or varnish stains, because when they dry, the resins in them set, or solidify. If you have used one of these, the only answer is a sixty-dollar belt sander from Sears, Roebuck & Co. or Montgomery Ward. But, boy, are they a great tool to have around the house. With one of them and a bandsaw, you are ready to open up shop. That's all I had when I started in this racket, and look at me now—a rich and famous author getting ready to go to Mexico in February!

You can't beat a winter in Mexico. They have a permanent weather report: chili today, but hot tamale!

7. Staining Plywood

So it doesn't come out looking like a flat zebra.

PLYWOOD is the worst problem a finisher ever has to face, because the dark streaks are real hardwood that will absorb hardly any stain at all, and the lighter areas in between are so soft and porous that they suck it in like a thirsty Arab. But there are a couple of things you can do to get around this and make even plywood look like something. Not like anything you want—but something.

One of the best things you can do is to decide that you want the piece to look like one of the dark woods. Such as walnut—which I think is your best bet—or dark-brownish or -reddish mahogany or dark antique cherry or ancient dark-brown antique pine. You can try for lighter or medium shades, and with the priceless techniques I am about to reveal, you will get reasonable results, but people will still say, "You've done a beautiful job—considering it's plywood." With the darker colors, you can really fool them.

Your first step is to do your best to equalize the absorption quotient of the darker orangey streaks and the paler wood areas in between. To do this, you *soak* the piece with shellac. Use orange shellac diluted with an equal part of denatured alcohol. Two coats. Now, when it is thoroughly dry, sand the whole surface with production paper wrapped around a flat block. This will take the shellac off the hard streaks so that stain can get at them, but it will not take it out of the porous wood into which it has sunk.

You can use regular clear shellac instead, but the orange helps to equalize the color between the hard and soft parts of the wood.

Now, when you brush on a stain, the hard grain will absorb what it can and the porous areas won't absorb much because of the shellac already in them.

Even more can be done, and that is to use a pigmented—and therefore semi-opaque—stain. Many oil stains have pigment in them, and this settles to the bottom of the can. Well, instead of stirring this up into all the liquid in the can, pour the top half or two thirds of the liquid off before stirring up the opaque pigment. Then brush this onto the plywood with a soft brush. When it is dry, spray it with a clear lacquer to stabilize the stain and pigment, and then build up your finish with additional coats of spray or brushed-on varnish.

For further obfuscation and concealment, you can also use a varnish stain, which is, in effect, colored varnish.

As I write this, I am sitting at an old card table I paid a dollar for at the local Goodwill Industries store. The cloth cover had been torn off, and underneath was dirty old plywood. I followed the procedure described, using a dark-walnut oil stain, and people won't believe it is plywood. Of course, I can't convince them that it is walnut either, but that's the way the cookie crumbles. You can't win them all.

8. Staining the Hardwoods

Such as maple and oak, which are so dense it's hard to get much stain into them. (But where there's a will, there's a way.)

IN earlier chapters I have talked about staining in relation to pine, because that is what almost all unfinished furniture is made of. And if you want to make something yourself, pine is the obvious wood to use, because it is easy to work with, stains so nicely, and is available in any lumberyard. (Incidentally, better-dried pieces—virtually warpfree—can be bought at millwork shops. These are places where windows and other house trimmings are made.)

But sometimes you will be faced with the problem of one of the harder woods—especially if you have stripped down an older piece of furniture or an antique. These woods fall into two groups. The first comprises oak and hickory, characterized by their large, open pores. Woods of the other group are dense, smooth, pale, and poreless: maple, birch, and the wood from fruit trees (except cherry, which isn't so hard; I discuss it in the next chapter).

Let's take oak first—and the same things go for hickory.

About the only oil stain that has any effect on oak

—and looks like anything—is walnut. Walnut stain will give it a brownish tone, instead of the natural yellow. The reason I say that walnut is the only color that looks like anything on oak (or hickory) is that the grain and figure of oak are so definite that even if you could get it cherry color, say, it would look like cherry-colored oak.

If you are really desperate—or maybe insanely determined—you can resort to spraying an alcohol-type stain onto the oak; that will give you a sort of translucent, colored, foggy surface. This is a pretty professional technique, of course, and involves owning and being skilled with a spray gun. (Or you can take a trip to New York City and get these stains in spray cans from the only place I know of that sells them. That is the great supplier to all professional finishers, H. Behlen & Bro., Inc. [the address is on page 40]. They have an incredible selection of stains, finishes, patching sticks, and everything related to wood finishing. Of course, they are in business to supply shops and factories, and so they don't care much about us home craftsmen or about doing business by mail. However, their store is open during the usual hours on the usual five days, and anyone is welcome then.)

A sprayed-on finish must be used over the sprayed-on stain. But after one coat of lacquer, you brush on varnish.

The pores in oak can present a problem if you are working with new wood or with an old piece that has been machine-sanded. You can buy a product for filling the pores so that you can get a smooth final finish, but it is the hardest thing I ever tried to do. I messsed around with it for threee days once, and never did get it to work. And I guess everybody else has the same trouble, which is why the so-called limed-oak finish was invented. The limed-oak finish results when you brush white paint on the wood and then wipe it off the surface—leaving it in the pores to accentuate them. This is most often done with oak that has been painted dark green or gray or black.

When it comes to other hardwoods—maple and so on—you can do a little more. To begin with, you aren't going to try to make these woods look like something else; you are going to accentuate the figure in them and darken them to one degree or another.

If you are using an oil stain, be sure the surface is freshly sanded. If you have removed an old finish with paint remover—or even a scraper—that is not good enough. A good hard sanding with fine production paper (not the finest, but one grade up) will open up the surface considerably so that it can absorb more stain.

This is also the area where the alcohol-type stains really come into their own. Oil stains will do just about anything you want on pine, but the spirit stains, as they are sometimes called, work much better on hardwood. Oil stains will do well on hardwoods to bring out the figure and darken them a little, but the spirit stains will get them as dark as you want. For where to find these and how to use them, see chapter 3, "Kinds of Stains."

9. Staining Dark Woods

Such as walnut, mahogany, and cherry. Anybody for teak, ebony, or rosewood?

NOT much unfinished furniture is made in woods other than pine. When we talk about the darker woods, we are involved with good factory-built or antique furniture that we have stripped down. With the exception of the great oak era in our history, walnut, mahogany, and cherry have always been the favorite woods of furniture makers—whether in a one-man shop or in a factory.

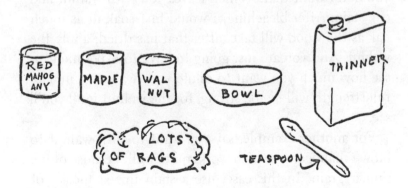

I put drawings like this in to make it look easy. Boy, are you in for a surprise!

There are a lot of reasons for this. In the first place, they have an even grain that doesn't split or chip when you are cutting or carving them. They are stronger than pine and don't dent with use. They have interesting figures that you can bring out by staining if you want to do so. Of course, stripping or sanding or scraping will often remove this stain, and you may want to restore it—or change it.

So let's say you have an old reddish-mahogany piece that you want to harmonize with your brown-mahogany pieces. First you will apply Clorox to the naked wood to remove as much of the old red stain as possible. This may work well or poorly, depending on what ancient stain was used. But it will work well enough in any case. Now you are going to have to experiment. Obviously, the wood isn't going to need any more red stain. And since maple stain has red in its orangey color already, you don't want that. Which leaves you with walnut and oak stain. After bleaching, I would first soak in as much oak as the wood will take. after that has dried, apply the walnut. And you are just going to have to experiment to see how much you want to dilute your walnut. I'm sure full strength will be too strong, for the walnut is all you'll see.

For another example, say you want to turn walnut to brown mahogany—which works quite well, because of the similar grain. In this case, use a stain mixed mostly of maple and, to this, add a little walnut and just a few drops of red mahogany.

To turn old-fashioned reddish cherry to modern brown cherry, you should use a mixture of walnut and oak. But, depending on the degree of red in your cherry, you are just going to have to experiment by mixing and trying out very small amounts to find your correct proportions.

Now as to teak, ebony, and rosewood, you aren't going to be able to do much with them. They are so hard and intensely colored that they will neither bleach nor take stain. With these woods—and similar rare ones like zebrawood—you are just going to have to learn to like them as they are. If you can't do that, you have two choices: you can spray dark walnut stain over them (see chapter 8, "Staining the Hardwoods") or you can paste veneeer over them.

Come to think of it, you can paint them with a color that approximates the wood you want them to look like. Or you can turn them—or turn anything else—into ebony: not by applying black paint but by making a stain with lampblack and lacquer thinner. This will leave some of the grain and pores showing, so that the wood still looks like wood—as it won't, very much, if you use black paint. Naturally, your first coat over this stain will have to be lacquer from a spray can to stabilize it.

10. *Applying a Shellac Finish*

The virtues and shortcomings of "old reliable" and the varnish makers' lie that you can't varnish over it.

SHELLAC starts out as a crust on some kind of tree in India made by some kind of bug chewing on the tree. After the crust is boiled down and the bugs are strained out, it ends up as brittle sheets or flakes, which arc dissolved in denatured alcohol. The resulting liquid is put in cans and sold to us as shellac. This is really true. When it is brushed onto furniture, the alcohol evaporates and you have a nice hard finish, which can be polished shiny as all get out or given a lovely soft glow by scuffing it with steel wool before waxing it.

Shellac has only one thing against it—which, on the other hand, is the best thing about it: it will immediately redissolve in alcohol.

The disadvantage in shellac's redissolving in alcohol is that you can't spill an alcoholic drink on it without having a disaster. When you wipe up the drink, the finish comes with it. Even water from the condensation on a glasss or vase will cause white spots and rings if allowed to stand too long. A coating of wax will delay the process for several hours, but probably not overnight. (Incidentally, such white spots can usually be removed, without penetrating the shellac, with just the breath of

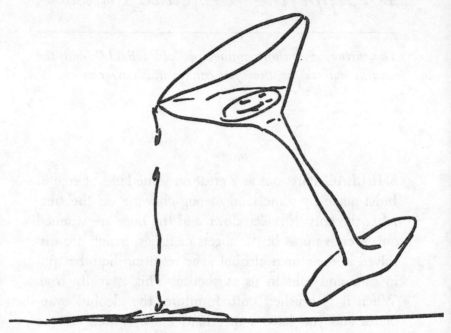

Shellac and alcohol don't mix—rather, they do, and that's just the trouble.

alcohol, ammonia, or lacquer thinner. Just wet a piece of soft cloth with one of those liquids, wring it out as hard as you can, and lightly brush the area with it. Rubbing the white spot with a paste of cigar ash and spit is another old-time remedy that usually works.)

Aside from the white-spot problem, however, the advantages of working with shellac are many:

1. Once you have thinned it down with denatured alcohol, it brushes on easily and quickly and doesn't make bubbles the way varnish sometimes does.

2. It is very fast-drying. You can put it on very thin to seal in a stain by mixing one part of shellac to four parts of alcohol, and it will be dry enough to cover with something else in half an hour.

3. You can mix it with only an equal part of alcohol or even less to get a built-up (thick) finish in a hurry—dry enough to rub down with fine steel wool in an hour.

4. If you don't like the results—say the stain under it is too light or too dark or the wrong color—you can wash it off with alcohol and rags in a couple of minutes and begin right away to work on staining or bleaching it.

5. It makes a good fast base for a final coat of varnish. In other words, you can stain, shellac, and varnish all in one evening and have the equivalent of three thin coats of varnish (the right way to put it on), which would take twenty-four hours to dry.

6. Finally, if you are a real experimenter, you can mix the alcohol-soluble powder stains (aniline dyes) into shellac to make a shellac sealer stain or the shellac equivalent of a colored varnish for obscuring an undesirable grain or figure in some wood you are faking-up.

To apply shellac, I would add three points to those just listed. First, use a soup bowl or small coffee can to mix shellac and alcohol. Pour about a cup of shellac in first, and add alcohol until you get the consistency you want. You decide what consistency you want by trying the mixture out on spare pieces of wood or on the undersides of tops and the backs of drawers.

Second, there is the problem of "blushing." This means that, in damp air, shellac will dry with a white haze. This can be prevented by using lacquer thinner instead of alcohol, or half alcohol and half lacquer thinner, to thin the shellac as it comes from the can.

Finally, always buy shellac in smallish cans—no bigger than a pint—and open a new can for each job. Once shellac has been exposed to the air and has been kept long enough, it loses its drying speed and gets gummy. I don't know why, but that's the way it is. It's cheap enough not to take chances with it. The same goes for denatured alcohol; buy that in quart cans, and use leftovers for brush cleaning.

11. *Applying a Varnish Finish*

Five easy steps to a perfect varnish finish—which means alcoholproof—if you'll promise not to read the directions on the can.

I have hardly ever read a word of truth, either in a book or on the side of a can, about how to apply varnish finish. Nobody else has, either, and that is probably why

Follow me, forsaking all others—and don't believe everything you read on the back of cans. Or on the fronts, either.

everybody thinks it is so hard to varnish. But if you do it the right way, it is easy. You don't have to worry about dust. You don't have to worry about bubbles. You don't have to worry about brush marks. You don't have to worry about its drying. Just follow the word of Grotz, and you can't go wrong.

But to keep things straight, let's first define varnish and what it does. What it is—nowadays—is a synthetic

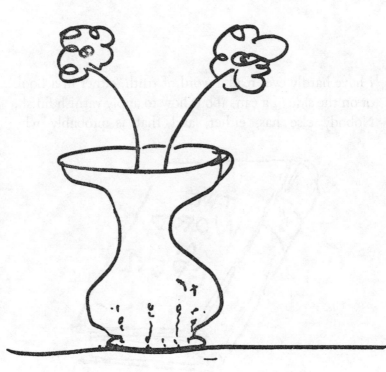

Some of the new plastic varnishes will even survive condensation from vases. But shellac sure won't.

resin that thins with mineral spirits or turpentine. And what it does is to dry hard. Once it has set, it won't redissolve in anything short of paint remover. It will stand firm and not white-spot under alcohol, fresh water, salt water, vegetable juices, lacquer thinner.

This was true of the old natural-resin varnishes, and the new synthetic-resin varnishes are even better. They are wildly impervious to almost anything, and the epoxy-based ones won't even come off with paint remover. You need a hammer and chisel.

Now, the first reason people have difficulty with varnish—up to the reading of books by me, that is—is that they aren't clean about it. But I guess they can be forgiven, because they haven't known how to get things clean. For instance, a piece of freshly sanded and dusted wood may look clean, but it is still full of minute specks of dust. For another example, no matter how well you think you have cleaned a brush after previous use, it still isn't really clean the way a new brush is. And then nobody ever thins varnish, because the makers never tell you on the can to thin it: they want you to use the varnish fast and buy more. Of course, they're cutting off their noses to spite their faces, because everybody ends up hating varnish.

Anyway, now you have the idea. The best way to tell you how to get a perfect varnish finish *easily* will be the old step-by-step approach. So here are the steps:

1 (What you need). Start out with a fresh can of varnish. It often does not keep, so don't be penny wise and pound foolish. Also buy a new brush for each varnish job. A medium-priced two-and-a-half-inch brush is what you want. Don't throw your money away on one of those expensive taper-bristle varnish brushes. They are

another racket, because they make varnish bubble worse than an ordinary brush. Finally, you will need a pint of mineral spirits and a soup bowl for mixing your varnish with the mineral spirits so that you never put your brush directly into the can.

2 (Preparing the surface). If the piece has already been shellacked or lacquered or sprayed or has had a coat of sealer-stain, all you have to do is rub it lightly with fine steel wool, dust it off well, and wipe it off with a tack rag. Now you are ready to go. (For what a tack rag is, see the end of chapter 1, "Preparation of the Surface.")

But if the piece is naked, sanded wood, you will have to give it a coat of shellac. This holds whether the wood has been stained or you are going to finish it in its natural color. Mix the shellac with four parts of alcohol for this

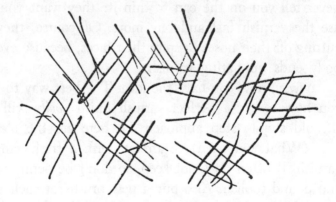

First scrub the varnish over the surface like this, and forget about the bubbles—I know what I'm talking about.

operation. It will be dry enough to varnish in fifteen minutes. (But go back and read chapter 10, "Applying a Shellac Finish," anyway.)

3 (Putting the varnish on). Pour about a cup of varnish into your bowl and add a dollop of mineral spirits. My idea of a dollop is a quarter of a cup. (Of course, not all varnish is of the same consistency, and so that's just a general rule. A safe one.)

Stir this up well with your brush. Now, let's say you are varnishing the top of a coffee table. With your brush dripping, I want you to cover the whole top, scrubbing the varnish in with short, hard, back-and-forth strokes. Really attack it, and raise all the bubbles and foam you want, but get it evenly distributed over the whole surface. (Since the varnish has been thinned, the bubbles are no longer any cause for worry.) Now check against a light to make sure there are no bare spots left. Finally, holding your brush at a fifteen-degree angle off the vertical, gently tip-off the varnish with strokes running from one end of the table to the other. This will take out the bubbles, and again, since the varnish has been thinned, your brush marks will also disappear in a few minutes.

4 (Drying). Let the varnish dry as long as the label on the can says. This is one of the few things on a label you can usually believe—if you are letting your pieces dry in a warm, dry room. (Direct sunshine out on the lawn is a real speeder-upper in the summer.)

5 (Rubbing). After the varnish is thoroughly dry,

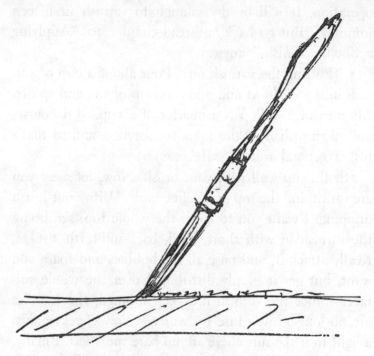

Tipping off carefully is the third secret, but it works only because you have thinned the varnish (in spite of what the stupid directions on the can say).

rub it hard with ooo-grade steel wool, having separated the pad into three pieces. Use straight strokes, following the direction of the grain at all times. There are some good brands of steel wool that stand up well and last a long time. But there is a lot of junk on the market that powders right away and gets little steel splinters in your fingers. The junk will work, but avoid it if possible. The piece is now ready to wax—whatever that means any more; we'll explore that in chapter 14, "The Great Wax and Polish Racket."

WARNING: One of the worst pitfalls an amateur can fall into is to ask a clerk in a paint-and-hardware store a question. Or for any advice about finishing furniture or about stains or about anything else. But, above all, never ask a clerk to recommend a good varnish, because all they know about is painting houses inside and out, and they will invariably try to sell you on how wonderful "spar" varnish is. Well, spar varnish is fine for outside work and for standing up under wind, snow, rain, and a hot summer sun. But that is because it is made not to dry all the way through, so that it can contract and expand with wide changes in temperature —from twenty below on a winter night to 130 in the sun on a summer afternoon.

But a gummy varnish on furniture you don't want. It never gets really dry, your steel wool will stick to it, and plates, if left long enough, will actually sink into it.

What you want are varnishes whose labels recommend them specifically for furniture and not for out-of-doors. Such varnishes will be labeled either *plastic* or *synthetic resin*. Any varnish that you find in a spray can will be one of these, and as I say in chapter 12, "Applying the Spray-can Finish," buy them all.

12. Applying the Spray-can Finish

As in Instant Furniture Refinishing, *which is another book entirely.*

I get so tired of hearing people knock sprayed finishes. Years ago, spraying got a bad reputation, because the early lacquers used in factory-production finishing were of a poor quality. They chipped easily and developed white rings from wet glasses.

But times have changed. The factory-sprayed finishes of today are as good as any hand-brushed-and-rubbed varnish of yesteryear—or of today, for that matter. The same goes for the kinds of sprays you get in cans these days. They are very, very good, and if you want an absolutely alcoholproof finish, all you need is the thinnest coat of varnish brushed over a lacquer finish. Any statements on your varnish can to the effect that this can't be done are just so much malarkey.

Before we get on with the uses of sprays, let's get it clear what I am talking about. I mean any of the spray cans labeled "Clear Finish" that you find in a paint-and-hardware store. They come under many trade names, and some are labeled "Acrylic," which is the same as saying good, clear lacquer. On virtually all of them the ingredients are listed in small print, and the "inert" one will be "Acrylic Ester Resin." O.K., they're still fast-drying, clear lacquers.

Now, once in a while you will find a varnish in a spray can whose label reads "Varnish" and notes that it takes several hours to dry. This is great stuff too, because it is as good as any canned varnish for a final alcoholproof coating over the "acrylic" lacquer. My advice is that, if you find any such cans, you buy them all, because it is a lot easier to spray on a varnish finish than it is to brush it on.

A lot of people will say they can't afford spray cans, but spray cans really aren't any more expensive than brush-on finishes when you stop to consider that their price is now down to about $1.50 a can. Besides, in comparing them with canned finishes, you can deduct the cost of brushes, thinner, and all the wasted remnants in cans that you don't use up. (Left-over varnish should never be used—see chapter 11, "Applying a Varnish Finish.")

When it comes to actual use, the spray can is as easy as heck—if you will do just one thing: Take your finger off the button after each sweep, and press it down to begin the next one. In other words, DON'T SPRAY CONTINUOUSLY, but spray with sweeps just as you would do with separate brush strokes. The idea is that your finger should come off the button while the can is still in motion. In this way you feather out the end of your spray stroke and AVOID THE PILE-UP OF LACQUER, WHICH WOULD RUN AND CAUSE DRIBBLES AND CURTAINS.

This is what happens if you don't lift your finger off the button at the end of each stroke!

The great advantage in spraying lacquer (or acrylic resins, if anyone insists) is that it dries in five to fifteen minutes. And I mean it dries enough to scuff down with steel wool in preparation for another coat or for a waxing of the final coat. When I was a lot younger and running a lot faster, I used to be able to go into a woman's house and "refinish" her dining-room table in an hour, using these cans. But for that kind of trick see my *Instant Furniture Refinishing.**

Another advantage of spray cans is that you can lay the stain on your naked wood pretty heavily when you need to get a dark color. To do this, it is best to use a padded rag to apply the stain, wiping it off lightly with the same rag. This leaves a lot of stain on the surface that a brush would pick up and blotch around.

* Doubleday & Company, Inc., Garden City, New York, 1966, $1.95.

But your first coat of clear spray will seal that down just the way you left it wiped.

Finally, there is no reason in the world that a final thin coat of varnish can't be applied over one or two coats of sprayed lacquer. The varnish manufacturers just say you can't on their cans, because they can't stand seeing anybody buying shellac or lacquer.

13. Linseed Oil and All That and Just Plain Wax

(Two chapters in one—a Grotz Double!)

THE linseed-oil finish is the old-time Early American special, and there isn't one thing the matter with it if you want a lovely soft finish that is durable and that darkens slowly with age—the way any good fake antique should. In fact, it is even great on Danish modern. The only thing is that it's a lot of work, and you know how that has gone out of style these days. Well, not exactly out of style. They've just changed the name. Now they call it "good therapy." If you need therapy, this is how you do it.

Prepare the bare wood surface by scuffing it—*with the grain*—with fine production paper, and clean off the excess dust. Now assemble the following:

> 1 quart of linseed oil
> ½-pint can of Japan drier
> 1 quart of mineral spirits (or turpentine)
> cotton rags

For your first application, mix one cup of linseed oil with a half cup of mineral spirits (or turpentine). Add

one overflowing tablespoonful of the Japan drier. Brush
this onto the wood until it won't absorb any more.
Then let the piece stand for an hour, and if any
dry spots have occurred, brush on some more. After
another hour, wipe off any of the mixture that hasn't
sunk into the wood. Wipe it off hard. Let the piece
dry in a warm place for a week.

You have your foundation for the finish, and now
the real therapy begins: you are going to have to rub
the piece down with more linseed oil once a week for
about three months. For these rubbings—each of which
will build up the surface finish a little more—you use this
mixture:

1 cup of linseed oil
1 overflowing tablespoonful of mineral spirits
1 level teaspoonful of Japan drier

This can be mixed in any quantity and kept in a jar
with a tight cover.

Each application calls for a hard rubbing with a pad
of cotton cloth. You apply the mixture as you would
a wax or polish, but you also spend about five minutes
rubbing it in hard. To finish it off, use your applicator
pad to wipe off excess oil. Wring the pad out as hard
as you can, and then wipe down the surface. Wring
the pad out again, and repeat.

It's a lot of work. But what you will get in the end
is a beautiful finish as good as varnish. Also it will

smell like linseed oil, and so everyone will know what a lot of good therapy you have had.

Of course, if you want to fake-out, there is a quicker way to get the same smell. Just apply a two- or three-coat shellac finish and top it off with a linseed-oil rub-down. This will give you the same soft glow as the real thing. And the same smell. Nobody will know. But *you* will, and haven't you enough things to feel secretly guilty about already?

WAX FINISH

The wax finish isn't used much, because it doesn't amount to much either. The problem is that wax will soften under anything greasy or oily, and it isn't much good on table tops except over a real finish. But it is all right on, say, the turned posts of a maple bed. Or small wooden objects or wood carvings.

Application is simple. You wipe on any good paste wax, let it dry well, and polish or buff it until it shines. Each coat will keep sinking into a soft wood such as pine, and so the effect is pretty dull. It really works well on very hard woods that have been fine-sanded very, very smooth. And since the wax won't sink into hardwood, with a couple of coats you can build up a good-looking if not very durable "finish." But you're really just fooling around.

14. The Great Wax and Polish Racket

Concerning all that baloney you see on television about "lemon oil" like Grandma used to use and "feeding the wood"—for which you'd need to have holes in your finish. Or your head.

But it's still good baloney, no matter how you slice it.

PEOPLE are always asking me what's the best wax or polish to put on their furniture. And I guess most of them expect me to come up with some old Yankee secret formula. But the truth is, there just isn't any, and those big wax companies that are always bringing out new products know what they're doing. They're inventing better things all the time. And when a big wax company comes out with a new spray wax called "Happy" or "Groucho" or "Cookoo," it's going to be the best thing to use on your furniture. It's going to repel dust and not show finger marks; it's going to stay clean and protect the finish and everything else better than what the company had invented as of last year.

It's the advertising that's insulting. The latest is a TV ad that shows a dopey bride and her wise old mother going crazy over a new "spray wax with lemon oil in it" (just like the good old days) that's "good for the wood."

In the first place, this is a silicone polish; it can be called a wax only by stretching the English language a little. And in the second place, there isn't now and never was any such thing as "lemon oil," as they perfectly well know. What used to be called lemon oil in Grandma's day was plain refined oil, just like the stuff that goes into your automobile. Instead of putting in mileage additives, they put in essence of lemon to make it smell good, while it gave your furniture a shiny but oily base for fingerprints and absorbed dust.

Finally, claims that any wax or polish is good for the wood or "feeds" it send me up the wall. How do people dare to say such things! A five-year-old child could see through them. What we are trying to do is to protect or beautify the *finish*, not dissolve it and get the wax or polish into the wood!

My recommendation is to use a modern spray silicone dressing, whether, ridiculously, it is called wax with lemon oil in it or not. But there are still a few things to be said in special cases for old-fashioned, hand-rubbed paste wax and even so-called "lemon oil."

A good paste wax, such as Butcher's or Simoniz, will stand up under hard use better than anything else. And for a bar top or comparable surface the paste waxes sold for use as an automobile finish are unquestionably the hardest and longest lasting. It is just a question of whether you want to go to the extra effort of hard hand rubbing.

The old lemon oil is really the old oil.

As to the "lemon oil" polishes—and these include the white, creamy polishes—I am well aware that these are what museums use on their priceless antiques. The reason is that even the thinnest coating of oil is a perfect moisture barrier. (Well, almost.) Oil keeps old finishes from drying out, soaks into cracks, and keeps moisture from moving in and out of the wood.

The white, oily polishes—creamy or thin—are actually oil emulsified with water. What this does is make the polish a cleaner. The water dissolves old candy and stuff on the surface, and the polishing cloth picks it up, at the same time leaving a film of oil. It's good—easy and fast.

Once in a while you see a polish that claims to have rare, expensive beeswax in it. Well, that's all right, so long as they don't put much of the gummy stuff in it, which I'm pretty sure they don't. I used to help my Uncle George try different mixtures for wax, and beeswax always ruined any batch we put it in.

Linseed oil is also used as a sort of polish-finish, but that becomes so complicated it needs a separate chapter —or part of one. See chapter 13, the first part, "Linseed Oil and All That. . . ."

15. Instant Antiques

Where the worm holes come from, and other aging techniques that fool 'em every time.

IN case you didn't know it, there's a lot of spoofing been going on about antiques for a long, long time—and matters have been getting even worse lately. So why should you be left out of the act? Besides, it's fun to fool your friends and relatives, and it's amazing how easy it is to make a brand-new unfinished piece of pine furniture into an antique overnight. Actually, it can be done in an evening.

The techniques are all pretty well known in the trade, and I've seen interior decorators in New York City doing the same things my Uncle George used to do in Vermont. What it amounts to is beating the piece up, getting it dirty, and then restoring it.

You can do this to any piece of furniture, but you'll get the best effect if you start out with a reproduction of an Early American piece. You see Early American reproductions in unfinished-furniture stores once in a while, but the best place to get them from is Francis Haggerty, down in Massachusetts. He has a terrific line of reproductions, from cobbler's benches to hutch cabinets, which he sells by mail. Send twenty-five cents for a catalogue to Cohasset Colonials, Cohasset, Massachusetts.

Even simple modern pieces can be made to look colonial in a hurry. For instance, a simple modern kneehole desk, chest of drawers, bedside table, or telephone table will work excellently.

If you're not in a hurry, one of the neatest tricks is to bury the piece in a nice mucky swamp or tidewater area for a few months—which, believe me, I know has been done. Works great. Loosens all the joints, rots the edges, and darkens the wood. All it needs is to be smashed around with a hammer a little, and the worm holes put in. Then you clean it up and finish it.

But you can achieve just about the same quality of antique in your workshop or garage or backyard on a nice sunny afternoon by following these nine steps:

1. Round the edges really well with rough production paper or a wood rasp. Work hard on the corners, the front edge of a desk top, the tops of rungs, and other places where wear would naturally occur.

2. Use a sharp hammer or a pinch bar (which is a

Secret weapons in the instant antiquer's arsenal.

short crowbar) to produce dents and nicks all over the thing. Smash the bottom of one leg, perhaps. (How should I know what a sharp hammer is. Am I a philosopher?)

3. Use a tire chain—rusty, if possible—to rumble the edges and beat the sides.

4. Now that the fibers have been broken in a lot of places, this is the time to get some dirt right into the

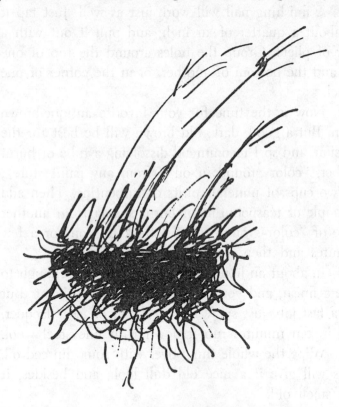

Clump of dirt—handy for rubbing old age into fake antiques.

wood. Any mud will do, but I prefer a clump of grass with nice fresh dirt, because it is handy for hard rubbing.

5. After the dirt has dried for five minutes, wipe the piece off well with dry cloths and go over the whole thing with fine or medium-fine sandpaper. (This step takes the longest; but do a complete job. No skipping.)

6. The worm holes go in now. One way is to blast a couple of rounds at the piece with bird shot at twenty feet. A finishing nail will work just as well. Just tap it in about a quarter of an inch, and pull it out with a pair of pliers. Group the holes around the top of one leg and the bottom of another, or in the corner of one panel.

7. Now is the time for your favorite antique-brown stain. But a good, dark, old brown will be best for the illusion, and so I recommend dissolving a tube of burnt umber, "color ground in oil" (from any paint store), in two cups of mineral spirits or turpentine. Then add a couple of teaspoonfuls of burnt sienna from another tube of "color ground in oil." Soak this on for a few minutes and then wipe off with a dry rag.

8. In about an hour, this stain will be dry enough to take a finish, and you can use anything you want. But for a fast job, just spray it with a can of clear lacquer, and in ten minutes rub it down with fine steel wool.

9. Wipe the whole thing over with some linseed oil. This will give it a nice old dull look, and besides, it will smell old.

END OF BOOK

Oh, all right, I'll explain it. I mean about the "sharp hammer." It's an old Jewish story my Irish grandmother used to tell me. It seems that these two bearded old boys were sitting at a table in the sunny window of a lower East Side cafeteria one afternoon. Skull caps and everything. Neither of them had said anything for about an hour, when Jacob looked down at his glass of tea and said, "You know, Sigmund, life is like a half a glass of tea."

Siggy thought it over for a while, and then he said, "Tell me, Jake, why is life like a half a glass of tea?"

Jake shrugged his shoulders and said indignantly, "How should I know, am I a philosopher?"

As my old Irish grandmother used to say, "Mozzeltof!"